Th Gauguin

Catherine de Duve

Embark on an exotic journey into the renowned painter's world of colour

KATE'ART EDITIONS

Around the world

Paul Gauguin was born in Paris on the 7th of June 1848. His mother, Aline Chazal, was born into a family that was descended from the Viceroys of Peru. His father, Clovis Gauguin, was a republican journalist. He decided to leave France after criticising *Louis Napoléon Bonaparte*'s victory in his newspaper. Peru here we come! Sadly, Gauguin's father died on their way there.

Martinique

Tahiti

Tahiti

Peru (Incas)

Young Paul lives in his uncle's lovely big house in Lima, the capital of Peru. He discovers a primitive country and culture. He fills his head with lots of exotic memories before moving back to Orleans at the age of six.

with Paul Gauguin

Gauguin wants to become a sailor. He longs to explore far away lands so that he can rediscover his childhood paradise. At 17, he joins the merchant navy before enrolling in the French navy. He sails for six years and goes around the world!

Brittany, France

Polynesia

Louis Napoléon Bonaparte (1808–73) became the first president of the French Republic on the 10th of December 1848. He restored the Empire (Second Empire) and became Emperor Napoléon III, France's last monarch. The massive changes engineered by Haussmann in Paris, were on his request. The french writer Victor Hugo opposed him in his writings.

Art Lover

Upon his return to France, Gauguin becomes a stockbroker on the Paris Stock Exchange. He discovers the Louvre Museum and begins to draw. At 25, Paul marries Mette-Sophie Gad, a young Danish woman he met whilst she was staying in Paris. They have five children together: Emile, Aline, Clovis, Jean-René and Paul-Rollon.

Paul Gauguin with his children, Clovis and Aline, in Copenhagen, 1885.

Gauguin is an art lover and visits the first impressionist exhibition in 1874*. He purchases work by Impressionist painters before becoming a painter himself and exhibiting alongside Pissarro, his guide and friend, as well as Cezanne*. Have you heard of them?

Gauguin is 34 and a family man when he decides to leave his job to dedicate himself to painting! He moves to Rouen shortly afterwards, close to his friend Pissarro, but his savings soon run out and the Gauguins are forced to move to Copenhagen, the capital of Denmark. Paul returns to Paris alone to paint. He exhibits his paintings with the Impressionists.

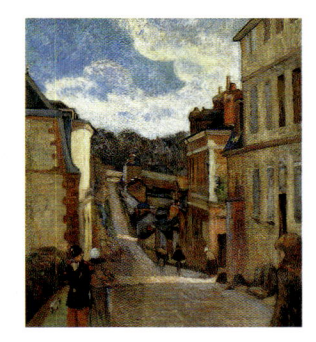

Rouen, 1884

It's your turn now to become an artist and paint your first masterpiece.

* To find out more, read *The Little Cezanne* and *Long Live Impressionism and Pointillism!* in the same collection: p.10-11.

Pont-Aven

Vertical Touches

In the summer of 1886, Gauguin moves to Pont-Aven, a small town in Brittany. He rents a room at the Gloanec bed & breakfast. He meets other artists there, including Charles Laval and Emile Schuffenecker who become his friends. He still draws inspiration from the Impressionist technique.

🔍 Look at the technique and brush stroke that Gauguin uses in this painting.

Far from the hustle and bustle of the town and civilisation, the artist concentrates on his art. He looks for primitive subjects and finds inspiration in popular beliefs, religion, superstition and rural life as well as from stained glass windows in churches, martyrs and women in traditional Breton costume.

The Calvary at Nizon

🔍 What are these Breton women doing? Look closely at their headdress, dresses, ruffs, aprons and wooden clogs. What is rustic about this painting?

Caribbean

In Gauguin's day, travelling was an adventure. Sea crossings were long and trying. Gauguin arrives exhausted in Panama in Central America with his friend Laval. He has no money left so he works as a labourer on the enormous *Panama Canal* project. The two friends decide to head to Martinique in the Caribbean where Gauguin has already been before. They stay there for a few months.

What are the women doing under the mango trees?

The Panama Canal was a gigantic and extremely complicated building site that took decades to complete (1881–1914), and opened up a maritime passage between two great oceans, linking the Atlantic to the Pacific.

The bluish coast and volcano can be seen in the distance bordering the bay of St. Pierre. The vegetation is composed of all shades of green and gold.
What colour is the Caribbean Sea?
This heavenly island looks deserted.
A lone cockerel pecks about.

Pencils, pens and paintbrushes at the ready! Draw your own tropical landscape.

Cloisonnism

"What to paint after impressionism?" Two years after his first stay there, Gauguin returns to Pont-Aven. He develops a new style with Emile Bernard! They simplify and synthesise shapes, do away with perspective and replace it with bold flat areas of solid colour. They call it *Cloisonnism* or *Synthetism*. The Pont-Aven group becomes known as the Synthetists.

Diagonal: A branch traces a diagonal and cuts the painting into two parts.

Symbolism: The Breton women kneel. Their eyes are shut and their hands joined in prayer. They are praying and imagining the story from the Bible that the priest told them about in his sermon, of Jacob wrestling with the angel. The painter is fascinated by popular beliefs that are coloured with superstition.

Cloisonnism* or *Synthetism found inspiration in stained glass and Japanese prints. Shapes are separated by heavy black outlines. Nowadays we use this technique in graphic novels, cartoons and animated films.

Émile Bernard

Whilst visiting his friend one day, Paul comes across a new painting that Emile has painted from memory. Back home, Gauguin starts work on an audacious composition that marks a turning point in the evolution of his style.

🔍

Compare Bernard's painting (below) to Gauguin's. Can you spot any similarities?

....

Red: The solid flat red background becomes an arena where the imaginary story (the sermon) takes place.

The Synthetists exhibit at the Café des Arts in Paris. However, Bernard accuses his friend of taking all the credit for the Pont-Aven group's inventions and their friendship comes to an end.

11

With Van Gogh

In 1888, Gauguin accepts an invitation from Vincent Van Gogh and heads to Arles, in the South of France. The two artists paint together but argue often. Two months later Gauguin leaves the country. Vincent is distraught. His dream of creating a community of artists collapses*. Van Gogh likes to paint out of doors, whereas Gauguin paints from memory in his studio. However, they both love vibrant and expressive colours.

🔍 Here's a self-portrait by Van Gogh. Compare it with the portrait Gauguin did of him (on the right) the same year.

* To find out more, read *Little Van Gogh*, in the same collection: p. 28-29.

🔍 Van Gogh sits facing his easel. What is he painting? Find the canvas he is busy painting amongst these details.

Iris *Buds* *Sunflowers*

🔍 Look for an artist's painting materials: easel, paintbrushes, palette, colours and canvas.

Tahiti

Portrait

In 1891, Paul Gauguin sails for Tahiti in Polynesia. He is still searching for that far away paradise where people live freely off the fat of the land like they did in the distant past. After more than two months at sea he arrives in Papeete and rents a small wooden house. He falls sick and is hospitalised. When he recovers he visits the archipelago. How stunningly beautiful it is! The turquoise lagoons, fish, flowers and vividly coloured fruit delight the artist. Gauguin feels very inspired. But life isn't easy. Occasionally, he receives commissions to paint a portrait, which help him to survive.

But the landscape with its violent, pure colours dazzled and blinded me. I was always uncertain; I was seeking, seeking... In the meantime, it was so simple to paint things as I saw them; to put without special calculation a red close to a blue. Golden figures in the brooks and on the seashore enchanted me. Why did I hesitate to put all this glory of the sun on my canvas? Oh! the old European traditions! The timidities of expression of degenerate races!

Extract taken from *Noa Noa* (1901), Paul Gauguin

Continue Gauguin's watercolour.

Noa Noa

Eternité de la Matière.—
Dialogue entre Téfatou et Hina (les génies de la terre - et la lune.

Hina disait à Fatou; "faites revivre (ou ressusciter) l'homme après sa mort.
Fatou répond: Non je ne le ferai point revivre. La terre mourra; la végétation mourra; elle mourra, ainsi que les hommes qui s'en nourrissent; le sol qui les produit mourra. La terre mourra, la terre finira; elle finira pour ne plus renaître.
Hina répond: Faites comme vous voudrez; moi je ferai revivre la Lune. Et ce que possédait Hina continua d'être; ce que possédait Fatou périt, et l'homme dût mourir.

13

Gauguin feels liberated in the tropics! He explores the archipelago and jots down his impressions in a notebook, using watercolours, wood engravings and collages to illustrate them. He calls his journal *Noa Noa* (1901), which means 'scented' in Tahitian. He is also interested in the traditions and legends of the ancient people of Polynesia, the Maori. However, Gauguin is sick and returns one last time to France in 1893. He is repatriated, taking with him in his trunks many paintings and sculptures. He exhibits in many places, notably Copenhagen, Brussels and Paris.

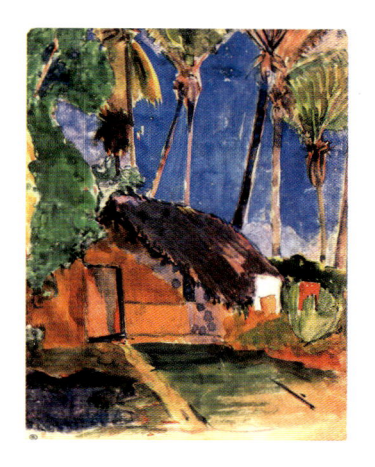

Just like Gauguin, write your explorer's diary, fill it with collages and find a suitable title for it:

Idol

Today is *Mahana no atua*! The day of the gods. Hina, the goddess of the moon is worshipped here. Gauguin represents her as a sculpture inspired from a photograph he has of Buddhist temples in Java. Women prepare the service, the sacred ritual…

Women wearing white wraps carry offerings of fruit or fragrant flowers on their head, while others dance around the idol. In front of us, multicoloured shapes shimmer on the water, like an abstract symphony.

Once back in Tahiti, Gauguin visits other islands, like Bora Bora. But the artist has a fractured leg that is not healing following a fight in Brittany. Gauguin's self-portrait with a yellow Christ on the cross symbolises his physical and moral suffering. Do you see it?

Selfportrait, 1889

🔍 **Observe the scene of the ritual. Replace the details in the painting.**

Reed pipe player

Goddess Hina

Ritual Dances

Offerings

A couple

Three bathers

Meditation

Now that he is back in Polynesia, Gauguin has a house built for himself by the sea. He starts working on a painting that is 4 metres long in which he expresses all his deep feelings. He seems to be painting a meditation: "Where do we come from? Who are we? Where are we heading?" The frieze is painted in a harmony of blues and Veronese green and reads from right to left. It represents the cycle of life.

🔍 **Find the different ages of life, from the infant to the old woman.**

Paul still lives in misery. He learns of the death of his daughter Aline. He is so distraught he tries to commit suicide by swallowing arsenic, a poison. he survives and eventually his life gets back to normal. He works at menial jobs to pay back his debts. Despite all his misfortune, he continues to paint visions of paradise.

It is indeed the outdoor life — yet intimate at the same time, in the thickets and the shady streams, these women whispering in an immense palace decorated by nature itself, with all the riches that Tahiti has to offer. This is the reason behind all these fabulous colours, this subdued and silent glow.

Paul Gauguin

Paradise

A white horse drinks from a river between the coiled branches of a tree in a tropical forest. He looks supernatural and wild. Can you hear his fiery neigh? Naked riders peacefully ride bareback. Man and beast live in harmony.

Is the horse white or green?

Imagine your own paradise and draw it.

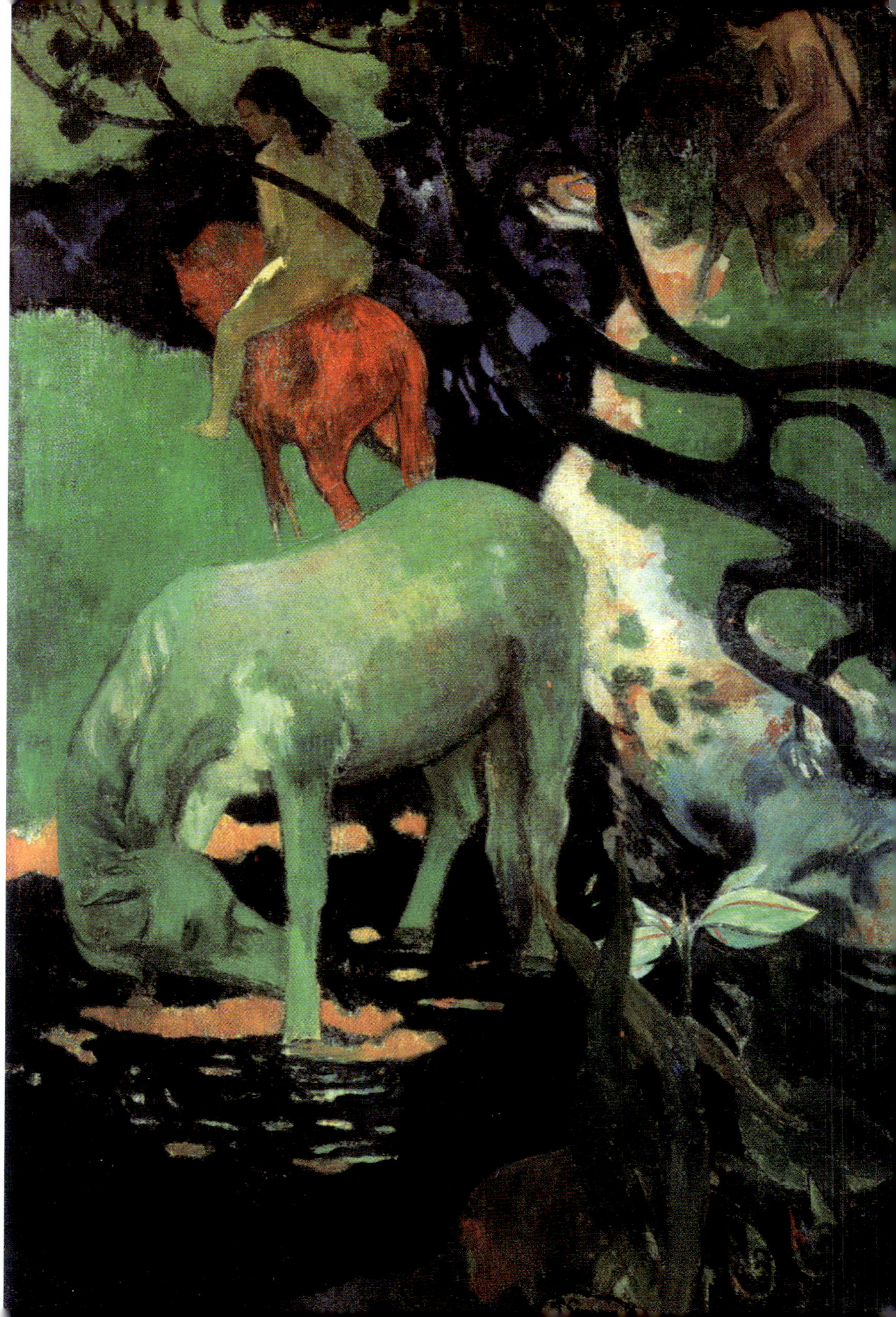

Wahines

Two graceful wahines sit on the ground. They have slipped a fresh flower into their black hair. What a lovely perfume! What makes them so still and dreamy? Gauguin loves these pacific people. Here he is painting his companion Teha'amana who serves as model for two of his figures. He makes a few versions of this painting.

Wahine is a Tahitian word that means "Tahitian woman".

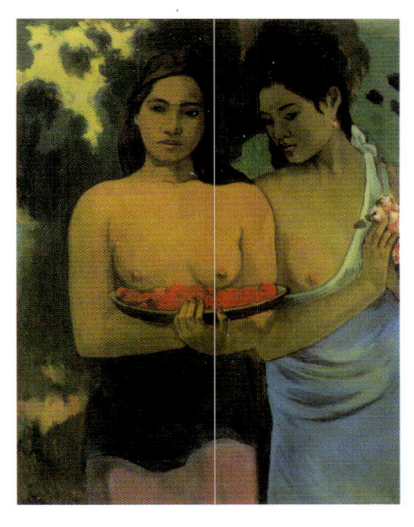

Two other women bring offerings of red fruit and pink mango flowers.

🔍 Compare the two versions. What differences do you see?

Colour

Two wahines bathe naked in the sea, nymph like. One of them holds her wrap around her waist and the other one cries for joy, her arms raised up to the sky. A fisherman approaches. Can you see him? The white waves are stylised just like the foliage and the tree trunk that is falling into the sea. One half of the painting is mainly composed of abstract shapes and vivid colours. Can you see them? It creates a decorative effect. Gauguin likes colour. What about you?

"That tree, how does it look to you?" Gauguin is said to have asked, then answered his own question. "It's green, isn't it? Paint it green then, the finest green on your palette. And this shadow, rather blue? Don't be afraid to paint it as blue as possible."

Compose a painting in the same way that Gauguin did, on either side of the line. One half realist, the other abstract and colourful.

An Island...

In 1901, Gauguin arrives in Atuona, an island in the Marquesas. He builds a house on stilts with workshops for sculpture and painting. The entrance is through a door that he made, decorated with statues and sculpted panels.

Wood carving, painted and gilded

🔍 What materials are these houses built of? Which one isn't from Tahiti?

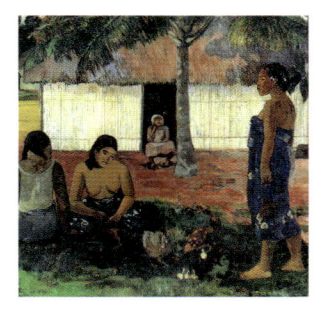

Draw your own thatched hut on your dream island just like Gauguin.

Inspirations

Turquoise waves break on a thin yellow sandbank. Horses wander on the vast bright pink beach. Further away, two riders tame their horses. They are dressed in bright colours, like jockeys preparing for a race. Gauguin was inspired by the paintings of Degas* depicting scenes from the Longchamp Hippodrome in Paris.

🔍 Compare both paintings. How did Gauguin (below) seek inspiration from Degas (on the right)?

🕊 **Edgar Degas** *(1834–1917) was an engraver, sculptor and impressionist painter. He developed his own style and worked in series and themes, such as dancers, women at their toilette and horses at the racetrack.*

* To find out more, read *Little Degas*, in the same collection.

Exhausted, Paul Gauguin dies on the 8th of May 1903 at the age of 55. He is buried in the Atuona cemetery in the Marquesas. Many painters like Picasso and Matisse will find inspiration in his art and his use of colour.

P Gauguin

Text and illustrations: Catherine de Duve
Concept and execution: Kate'Art Editions
Graphic design: Carole Daprey
Adapted into English by: Kerry-Jane Lowery

Paul Gauguin
AMSTERDAM: Rijksmuseum Vincent Van Gogh: *Mango Gatherers*, 1887: p. 2, p. 8; *Van Gogh Painting Sunflowers*, 1888: p. 13 – **BOSTON:** Museum of Fine Arts: *"Where Do We Come From? What Are We? Where Are We Going?"*, 1897: p. 20–21 – **BRUSSELS:** The Royal Museums of Fine Arts of Belgium: *Conversation in the Fields. Pont-Aven*, 1888: p. 3, p. 6; *Breton Calvary*, 1889: p. 7 – **CHICAGO:** The Art Institute of Chicago: *Mahana no Atua (Day of the Gods)*, 1894: p. 2, p. 18–19; *"No te aha oe riri?" (Why Are You Angry?)*, 1896: p. 28 – **DRESDEN:** Gemäldegalerie Neue Meister: *"Quelles nouvelles?" (What News?)*, 1892: p. 24 – **EDINBURGH:** National Gallery of Scotland: *Vision After the Sermon or Jacob Wrestling with the Angel*, 1888: back cover, p. 10–11; *Tropical Vegetation, Martinique*, 1887: p. 9 – **MADRID:** Musée Thyssen-Bornemisza: *Mata Nua*, 1892: inside cover; *Rue Jouvenet à Rouen*, 1884: p. 5 – **MERION:** Barnes Fondation: *Portrait of Loulou*, 1890: p. 14 – **MINNEAPOLIS:** Minneapolis Institute of Arts: *Mountains in Tahiti*, 1893: p. 2, p. 14 – **MÜNCHEN:** Neue Pinakothek: *Four Breton Women*, 1886: p. 7 – **NEW YORK:** Metropolitan Museum of Art: *Tahitian Women*, 1899: cover, p. 25 – **PARIS:** Musée d'Orsay: *Noa Noa, landscape*: p. 3, p. 28; *White Horse*, 1898: p. 22–23; *Tahitian Women (On the Beach)*, 1891: p. 24, p. 25; *Tahitian Woman's Head (facing)*, around 1892: p. 28; *Carved panel from La Maison du Jouir (The House of Pleasure)*, 1902: p. 29; *Carved panel "Find love and you will find happiness"* 1902: p. 29 | The Louvre Museum, Cabinet des dessins: *Ancient Maori Cult*: back cover, p. 15, p. 16 – **WASHINGTON, D.C.:** National Gallery of Art: *"Fatata te Miti". By the Sea*, 1882: p. 26–27 – **Private collection:** *The Siesta*, 1893: p. 28 – **Stavros Niarchos Collection:** *Riders on the Beach*, 1902: p. 30.
Photographs: *Gauguin in 1888*: p. 2; *Gauguin with his palette*: p. 4; *Paul, Clovis and Aline Gauguin in Copenhagen*, 1885: p. 4; *Gauguin in Paris*, around 1893–94: p. 31.

Émile Bernard
Private collection: *Breton Women in the Meadow*, 1888: p. 11.

Vincent Van Gogh
AMSTERDAM: Rijksmuseum Vincent Van Gogh: *Blossoming Almond Tree*, 1890: p. 13; *Self portrait*, 1888: p.12; *Sunflowers*, 1888: p. 13; *Vase with Irises*, 1890: p. 13.

Edgar Degas
BOSTON: Museum of Fine Arts: *Racehorses at Longchamp*, 1871–74: p. 30.

We would like to extend out thanks to all the people who participated in the creation of this book.

Books by Kate'Art Editions are available in various languages:
French, English, Dutch, German, Spanish, Japanese, Danish and Russian

Go to www.kateart.com and its online boutique